Old Sheffield Plate
and Close Plate
Makers' Marks
from 1784

EPNS
Electroplated Nickel Silver, Old Sheffield Plate and Close Plate Makers' Marks
from 1784

George Mappin

foulsham
LONDON • NEW YORK • TORONTO • SYDNEY

foulsham

The Publishing House, Bennetts Close,
Cippenham, Berkshire, SL1 5AP, England

ISBN 0-572-02419-3

Printed in Great Britian

CONTENTS

OLD SHEFFIELD PLATE AND ELECTROPLATE

One of the problems with identifying plated items is that there is no single source of information on the makers' marks. Add to this the fact that some marks are not registered at all and checking every mark becomes impossible. Therefore, while every effort has been made to ensure accuracy, it is not possible to go back to source to verify every mark.

Old Sheffield Plate

Old Sheffield Plate was made by a different process from electroplate and the marks referring to Old Sheffield Plate are indicated in the book by (OSP).

Old Sheffield Plate was invented in the middle of the eighteenth century and its manufacture continued until about the 1860s, by which time electroplating was well established. It was made by fusing a layer of silver on to copper. The designs used by the manufacturers were copied from popular silverware and much Old Sheffield Plate was made by silversmiths. The plate has a faint glow with a blueish tinge and is less dull than electroplated silver.

The words 'Best Sheffield Heavy Plating' were only used after 1820. Between 1773 and 1784 Old Sheffield plate has no marks as manufacturers were forbidden to mark their goods to prevent them from passing them off as silver. Later items, however, may also not carry a mark.

'Sheffield Plated' is only used on electroplated items.

Close Plate

Close plating was the only way of silver plating steel. Electroplating steel was not successful because the adverse reaction of the electrolyte on the base metal made it rust.

The article was made in steel and completely finished. It was then dipped in sal ammoniac, which acted as a flux, and then into molten tin, so that it was completely covered.

Silver foil was cut into the shape of the article and put into position. A heated soldering iron was then rubbed over its surface, causing the underlying tin to melt and unite the silver and steel.

Close plating was a Sheffield and Birmingham trade. Samuel Roberts, a Sheffield manufacturer, took out a patent for the manufacture of Close Plate spoons and forks in 1789, but most of the items found now date from the nineteenth century or the period up to 1914. The main items made in Close Plate were those which required more strength than would be found in Old Sheffield Plate. They include spurs, buckles, candlesnuffers, nutcrackers, skewers, marrow scoops, fish slices and, of course, dessert knife blades, ladles, spoons and scissors.

Most Close Plate items are marked. An Act of Parliament of 1784 laid down that Old Sheffield Platers and Close Platers working in Sheffield and an area of 100 miles radius around it (which included Birmingham) had to register their marks at the Sheffield Assay Office.

Records are complete until the mid 1830s when this Act became a dead letter. Close Platers' marks usually consist of a number of different shields containing the maker's initials and registered device, sometimes struck twice, and the letters PS for plated steel.

Electroplate

Electroplating or silver plating was perfected in 1842 by Elkington & Co. of Birmingham. Articles made of copper, Britannia metal, nickel silver, nickel, brass or British plate were used as the base and coated with a layer of pure silver. The item to be plated was attached to a negative pole and submerged in a solution of potassium cyanide. The positive pole was attached to a 100 per cent pure silver sheet. A low-voltage current was then passed through the solution. The silver sheets acted as a cathode producing silver ions which passed into the solution. These were drawn to the article, acting as an anode, adhering to its surface. A thicker layer was produced the longer the article was immersed in the charged solution. The quality of the product is partly dependent on how clean the Portland cement-lined vat containing the solution was kept, as foreign bodies in the solution caused imperfections in the plating. Once removed from the solution, the article was hammered over its surface to ensure that the silver coating had adhered properly, then burnished.

Many manufactuers of Old Sheffield Plate moved over to the new process and marked their wares with their stamp. In general, marked English EPNS is from Sheffield, while unmarked English EPNS is from Birmingham. However, usually only the teapot in a teaset was marked so do not be misled by unmarked cups, etc.

Base Metals

Nickel Silver
An alloy of copper, zinc and nickel, nickel silver was discovered to be the best base for electroplating and is still used today. Worn areas show the base metal as silvery-grey. Items often have EPNS or EPGS (electroplated German silver, named as nickel was first mined in Saxony) stamped on the base; or they may display EP, NS or GS.

British Plate is a form of nickel silver and BP is usually marked on the base of goods made of British Plate.

Copper
A popular base metal at the beginning of electroplating, copper became less popular as it was softer than nickel silver and because when the silver coating began to wear away, the base metal showed through as an unsightly orangey-red.. Silver-plated copper wares are usually from the early to mid Victorian period and often have EP stamped on the base.

Britannia Metal
Britannia metal is a form of hard pewter developed about 1770 as a cheap alternative to Old Sheffield Plate. It was then found that it made a good base for electroplating and plating on Britannia metal started in 1845. By 1870, however, the increasing burden of labour costs led to the production of poor quality wares made of thin gauge metal

with only a light coating of silver. After 1855, EPBM is often stamped on the base of Britannia metal items. Pewter goods are collectible in their own right.

Design Registration Marks

Some metal wares may be dated approximately if their design was registered.

Diamond Registration Marks

A diamond-shaped impressed registration mark dates the article as 1843-83 or an impressed registration number from 1884.

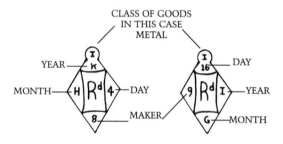

Year Letter Codes 1842-67

A	1845	J	1854	S	1849
B	1858	K	1857	T	1867
C	1844	L	1856	U	1848
D	1852	M	1859	V	1850
E	1855	N	1864	W	1865
F	1847	O	1862	X	1842
G	1863	P	1851	Y	1853
H	1843	Q	1866	Z	1860
I	1846	R	1861		

Year Letter Codes for 1868-83

A	1871	I	1872	U	1874
C	1870	J	1880	V	1876
D	1878	K	1883	W	1878
E	1881	L	1882	X	1868
F	1873	P	1877	Z	1879
H	1869	S	1875		

Months

The months were the same for both series.

A	December (except 1860)
B	October
C	January
D	September
E	May
G	February
H	April
I	July
K	November and December 1860
M	June
O	January
R	August and 1–19 September 1957
W	March

Date

The date of the month was marked simply as the number.

Registration Numbers

From 1884, registration numbers took over from the diamond registration mark.

1884	1–19753	1895	246975–268391
1885	19754–40479	1896	268392–291240
1886	40480–64519	1897	291241–311657
1887	64520–90482	1898	311658–331706
1888	90483–116647	1899	331707–351201
1889	116648–141272	1900–09	35120–550999
1890	141273–163766	1910–19	552000–673749
1891	163767–185712	1920–29	673750–751159
1892	185713–205239	1930–39	751160–837519
1893	205240–224719	1940–49	837520–860853
1894	224720–246974		

Makers' and Other Marks

Knowing the maker can help to establish the date of an article as you can ascertain when that company was producing goods.

Most Sheffield platers stamped their initials on to their wares, but some used their surname or full name. In order to mimic sterling silver, makers often punched their initials in a sequence of four punches, and marks were usually in intaglio, that is punched with the letters in relief. If they did not have the required number of initials, they would commonly add a fourth, often 'S', at the end.

Some marks use an 'I' instead of a 'J' in the company initials.

Trade Marks
Trade marks could be registered from about 1878.

A1
This is stamped on some wares to indicate the best quality but has no real significance.

Electroplated
Sometimes stamped on electroplated wares.

England or Made in England
'England' is commonly found on goods between 1890 and 1920 but never before that time.

'Made in England' is sometimes found on goods made after about 1920.

Crown inside a Shield
This denotes that a product was made before 1897. It was designed to mimic the Sheffield silver crown but its use was banned in about 1897.

Numbers or Letters

A single number may denote the capacity in half pints, although it can also denote a variation in size or a particular style or even the workman's number. A single or pair of letters are frequently the workman's initials.

HOW TO USE THIS BOOK

This book is designed to help you identify marks found on EPNS and Old Sheffield Plate. The organisation of the information is based on the fact that the mark itself is your starting point.

The marks are not necessarily shown to scale. In some cases, detail has been lost due to wear and tear. Different companies with the same surname may or may not be related.

Old Sheffield Plate is marked (OSP).

Close Plate is marked (CP).

The marks have been organised in two sections.

The first section includes all those marks which contain initials, names or words.

- The marks under each letter are listed with the initials first, in alphabetical order where relevant, followed by the names and words in alphabetical order.
- Where the mark contains initials and one of those initials is clearly dominant, the mark has been listed under the dominant letter.
- Where the mark contains initials and none is dominant, the mark has been listed under the first initial letter, reading from left to right. This is because the initials do not always relate readily to the maker's actual name.
- Where a full name is provided in the mark, it has been listed under the initial letter of the surname.

The second section contains marks which are purely pictorial and contain neither initials nor names. They are grouped into images with a similar theme, then into alphabetical order by the name of that general type of image, such as 'bell' or 'hand'.

Charles James Allen &
Sidney Darwin
Sheffield
1893 ...

 Charles James Allen &
Sidney Darwin
Sheffield
1879 c. ...

 Charles James Allen &
Sidney Darwin
Sheffield
1893 ...

 Armstrong & Scott
Birmingham
1894 ...

 T. Aston & Son
Birmingham
1893 ...

 A.J. Beardshaw & Co.
Sheffield
1893 ...

 A. Beardshaw & Co.
Sheffield
1869 ...

 Alfred Browett
Birmingham
1855 c. – 1896

 Browett, Ashberry &
Co.
Birmingham
1897 ...

A.J. Beardshaw & Co.
Sheffield
1893 ...

A. Beardshaw & Co.
Sheffield
1879 c. ...

Briddon Brothers
Victoria Plate Works,
Sheffield

Atkin Brothers
Sheffield
1853 ...

Ashforth Ellis & Co.
Sheffield
1770

Arthur E. Furniss
Sheffield
1870 c. ...

George Bowen & Sons
Birmingham
1890 c. ...

Francis Higgins Jr;
Portland Co. Ltd
London & Clapton Mills
1859–1867

Martin Brothers & Co.
Sheffield

 A. Hatfield
Sheffield
1808   (CP)

 Thomas H. Daniel &
Thomas R. Arter
Birmingham
1882 c.–1896

 Jehoiada Alsop Rhodes
Sheffield
1872 c.–1888 c.

 Silber & Fleming
London
1884–1898

 Silber & Fleming
London
1884–1898

 Arthur Willis
Sheffield
1897 ...

 Henry Williamson
London

 H. Schurhoff & Co.
Birmingham

 Hills, Menke & Co.
Birmingham

17

Lee & Wigfull
John Street Works,
Sheffield

ALBION SILVER

Thomas Aldridge
London
1865 c. ...

THOMAS ALDRIDGE
57 BROMPTON ROAD
LONDON

Societe Anonyme des
Converts Alfenide
Paris

John Round & Sons Ltd
Sheffield
1880 c ...

James Allan & Co.
Sheffield
1849–1855

James Allan
Sheffield
1855–1872

JAMES ALLAN
SHEFFIELD

J. Allgood
Sheffield
1812   (CP)

ALL GOOD

E. Allport
Sheffield
1812   (CP)

Joseph Gilbert
Sun Works,
Birmingham

ALMADA SILVER

	Harrison Brothers & Howson *Sheffield* 1898 c ...
	Viners *Sheffield* 1925–1974
	Daniel & Arter *Globe Nevada Silver Works, Birmingham*
	Rosing Brothers & Co. *London*
	Perry & Company Ltd *Birmingham*
	William Hutton & Sons *Sheffield* 1886 c.–1893
ARCAS	Cowper-Coles, Cowper Bickerton *London*
	Daniel & Arter *Globe Nevada Silver Works, Birmingham*
ARGENTINA SILVER *Joseph Gilbert*	Joseph Gilbert *Sun Works, Birmingham*

Gilding & Silvering Co. *Middlesex*	**ARGOSY SILVER**
Solomon Lewis Gorer *Middlesex*	**ARGOSY SILVER**
Arnold & Lewis *Manchester* 1875 c. ...	**ARNOLD & LEWIS MANCHESTER**
Philip Ashberry *Sheffield* 1845 c.–1855	**PHILIP ASHBERRY SHEFFIELD**
Philip Ashberry & Sons *Sheffield* 1856–1860 c.	*PHILIP ASHBERRY & SONS BEST ELECTRO PLATE SHEFFIELD*
Philip Ashberry & Sons *Sheffield* 1861 ...	**PHILIP ASHBERRY & SONS SHEFFIELD**
Philip Ashberry & Sons *Sheffield*	
Philip Ashberry & Sons *Sheffield* 1861–1915	
G. Ashforth & Co. *Sheffield* 1784 (OSP)	

Ashley
Sheffield
1816

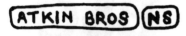 Askew
Nottingham
1828

 Atkin Brothers
Sheffield
20th Century

 Perry & Co. Ltd
Birmingham

Broadhead & Atkin
Sheffield
1846–1853

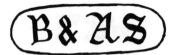

Biddle & Collingwood
Birmingham
1875 ...

Brookes & Crookes
Atlantic Works
Sheffield (cutlery only)

Brown & Clark
Birmingham

Benetfink & Co.
London
1895 c...

Boulton & Fothergill
Birmingham
1764 (OSP)

Boardman, Glossop & Co.
Sheffield
1847–1894

Boardman, Glossop & Co.
Sheffield & London
1895 ...

Boardman, Glossop & Co.
Clarence Works
Sheffield

Henry Bourne &
Daniel J. O'Neill
Birmingham
1881–1886

BB

Henry Arthur Goodall
London

Barker Brothers
Birmingham
1886–1896

Briddon Brothers
Victoria Plate Works
Sheffield

Briddon Brothers
Sheffield
1863–1910

Chantrill & Co.
Birmingham

The Birmingham Guild
of Handicrafts Ltd
Birmingham
1897 …

Barnett Henry
Abrahams
London
1890 …

B.J.R&S

B.J. Round & Sons
Birmingham
1900 …

James Pinder & Co.
Sheffield
1877–1894

Badger, Worrall &
Armitage
Sheffield

Bingley, George Bower
Sheffield

Ihlee & Horne
London

W. Banister
Birmingham
1808

Silverston, Isaac & Co.
Birmingham

Henry Barnascone
Sheffield
1868 c.–1883 c.

Henry Barnascone & Son
Sheffield
1884 ...

Barnet

Z. Barraclough & Sons
Leeds
1887 ...

 H. Samuel & Sons
Manchester

 Beach & Minte
Birmingham

 G. Beldon
Sheffield
1809

Beldon, Hoyland & Co.
Sheffield
1785
OSP

BENETFINK & Co.
London
1880 c ...

J.W. Benson
London

 Daniel & Arter
*Globe Nevada Silver
Works, Birmingham*

 H. Best
Sheffield
1814

Best & Wastidge
Sheffield
1816

Henry Biggin & Co.
Sheffield
1880–1884

**HENRY
BIGGIN & CO.
SHEFFIELD**

W. Bingley
Sheffield
1787

Birts & Son
Woolwich

Thomas Bishop
Sheffield
1830

Arthur Culf
Sheffield

William Page & Co.
Birmingham

Slack & Grinold
Bath Works, Sheffield

M. Boulton & Co.
Birmingham
1784

BOVAL	James Woolley, Sons & Co. *Manchester*
	Joseph Bradshaw *Birmingham* 1822 c.
	J. Bradshaw *Birmingham* 1822
	Daniel & Arter *Globe Nevada Silver Works, Birmingham*
BRENADA SILVER J. R. McC.	James Robert McClelland *Sheffield*
WM BRIGGS&Co SHEFFIELD	William Briggs & Co. Sheffield 1876–1900
	Atkinson Brothers *Mill Works, Sheffield*
	Philip Ashberry & Sons *Sheffield* 1861 ...
	Browett, Ashberry & Co. *Birmingham*

Browett, Ashberry & Co.
Birmingham
1897 ...

Benjamin Grayson &
Son
Sheffield
1871 ...

Brittain, Wilkinson &
Brownhill
Sheffield
1785   (OSP)

Broadhead & Atkin
Sheffield
1843–1853

Rogers Broadhead & Co.
Sheffield
1853–1900

Cooper Brothers &
Sons Ltd
Sheffield
1867–1964

Joseph Brown
Sheffield
1849–1867

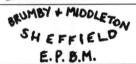

Brumby & Middleton
Sheffield
1889–1897

Daniel & Arter
*Globe Nevada Silver
Works, Birmingham*

John Moreton & Co.
Wolverhampton,
Sheffield & London

T. Butts
Birmingham
1807 c.

BUXTON &
RUSSELL

Edwin James Buxton
& Samuel Russell
Sheffield
1852–1860

Joseph Elliot & Sons
Sheffield
1890 c ...

Creswick & Company
Sheffield

Carnelly & Co.
Birmingham
1867–1885 c.

Creswick & Co.
Sheffield
1855 c.–1887

Creswick & Co.
Sheffield
1863–1887

Culf & Kay
Sheffield
... 1896

C. Boardman
Sheffield

Roberts
Sheffield
1879–1892

Cooper Brothers &
Sons Ltd
Sheffield
1895 c. ...

	George Edwards *Glasgow*
	Charles Ellis & Co. *Sheffield*
	Muirhead & Arthur *Glasgow* 1883 c. ...
	Charles Howard Collins *Birmingham* 1889 ...
	Hawksworth, Eyre & Co. *Sheffield* 1850 c. ...
	Cartwright, Hirons & Woodward *Birmingham* 1853–1859
	Christopher Johnson & Co. *Sheffield* 1896 ...
	Levesley Brothers *Central Works,* *Sheffield*
	Sissons *Sheffield* 1855–1891

C

Lockwood Brothers Ltd.
Sheffield
1898 c. ...

C ✝ X

Levetus Brothers
Birmingham

Hawksworth, Eyre &
Co. Ltd
Sheffield
1900 c. ...

J. F. Causer
Sheffield
1824   (OSP)

Thomas S. Richards & Co.
Birmingham

T. Cheston
Sheffield
1809

T. Child
Sheffield
1812   (OSP)

Christofle & Company
Paris

Land
Sheffield
1920–1944

TRADE CIVIC MARK
E. P. B. M.

Land
Sheffield
1945–1977

John Clarke & Sons
Sheffield
1895 ...

CLARKS

JUBILEE GOLD

John Clark
Birmingham

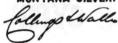

W. Coldwell
Sheffield
1806   (OSP)

Collings & Wallace
Birmingham

George Richmond
Collis & Co.
Birmingham & London
1873–1893

John Shaw & Sons,
Ltd.
Wolverton

C. G. Cope
Sheffield
1817   (OSP)

J. Corn & J. Sheppard
Birmingham
1819   (CP)

Joseph Deakin & Sons
Sheffield
1856–1864

J. Cracknall
Sheffield
1814

Creswick & Co.
Sheffield

CRESWICK & C⁰.

T. & J. Creswick
Sheffield
1811 ...

Judd & Co.
London

THE CYPRUS

 John Gilbert & Co. Ltd
Birmingham & London
1879–1890

 Thomas H. Daniel &
Thomas R. Arter
Birmingham
1897 ...

 Davenport & Bray
Sheffield
1871–1874 c.

 William R. Deykin &
Walter A. Harrison
Birmingham
1895 ...

 Frederick Derry &
Henry Jones
Birmingham
1861–1866

 William R. Deykin &
Sons
Birmingham
1854–1895

 J. Dixon & Sons
Sheffield
1835   (OSP)

 J. Dixon & Sons
Sheffield
1835

 J. Deakin
Sheffield
1855–1891

D. Not attributed 1760 (OSP)	
Dawson & Co. *Birmingham* 1897 ...	
Fenton Brothers *Sheffield* 1897–1910 c.	
J. Davis *Sheffield* 1816 (OSP)	
James Deakin & Sons *Sheffield* 1871–1900 c.	**JAMES DEAKIN & SONS** **CUTLERS SHEFFIELD**
Joseph Deakin & Sons *Sheffield* 1856–1864	JOSEPH DEAKIN & SONS SHEFFIELD
Joseph Deakin & Sons *Sheffield* 1864–1889	JOSEPH DEAKIN & SONS SPRING STREET WORKS SHEFFIELD
Deakin Smith & Co. *Sheffield* 1785 (OSP)	
Brookes & Cookes *Sheffield*	

Mark	Maker
	T. Dixon & Co. *Sheffield* 1784 (OSP)
JAMES DIXON&SONS SHEFFIELD	James Dixon & Sons *Sheffield* 1851 ...
	James Dixon & Sons *Sheffield* 1835 (OSP)
	James Dixon & Sons *Sheffield* 1879 ...
	James Dixon & Sons *Sheffield* 1890 c. ...
	James Dixon & Sons *Sheffield* 1835 c. (OSP)
	James Dixon & Sons *Sheffield* 1835 (OSP)
	James Dixon & Sons *Sheffield* 1835 (OSP)
	I. Drabble & Co. *Sheffield* 1805 (OSP)

D

G. B. Dunn
Birmingham
1810

Frederick Barnes & Co.
London, Birmingham
& Sheffield

Frederick Barnes & Co.
London, Birmingham
& Sheffield

John James Durrant
London
1874–1897

	Elkington & Co. *Birmingham* 1840–1897	
	Elkington & Co. *Birmingham* 1898–1899	
	Elkington & Co. *Birmingham* 1900 ...	
	Ellis & Co. *Birmingham* 1896 ...	
	Elkington & Co. Ltd *Birmingham*	
	Elkington & Co. Ltd *Birmingham*	
	Elkington & Co. Ltd *Birmingham*	
	Elkington & Co. Ltd *Birmingham* 1865 ...	
	E. Bradley *Sheffield*	

39

Edwin Blyde & Co.
Sheffield
1872 ...

Arthur E. Furniss
Sheffield
1872 ...

Haseler Brothers
Birmingham
1888 ...

E. J. Makin
Sheffield

Elkington, Mason & Co.
Birmingham

Elkington, Mason & Co.
Birmingham
1842–1864

Mappin Brothers
Queens Works,
Sheffield & London

Mappin Brothers
Queens Works,
Sheffield & London

A. Hodd & Sons
Middlesex

A. Hodd & Sons
Middlesex

   Wilson & Davis
London & Sheffield

 W. R. Humphreys & Co.
Sheffield
1889 c. ...

 Robinson & Company
Sheffield

    Ebenezer Stacey & Sons
Sheffield
1870 c.–1900 c.

 E.S. Wells
Birmingham
1899 ...

T.W. EATON & CO. SHEFFIELD T.W. Eaton & Co.
Sheffield
1899 ...

 EGLENTINE F. Eglington
Staffordshire

Electro-Imperial. **F.W.** Frederick Whitehouse
Lion Works,
Birmingham

41

The Potosi Company
Birmingham

Elkington & Co. Ltd
Birmingham
... 1870 c.

Elkington & Co. Ltd
Birmingham

Elkington & Co. Ltd
Birmingham

W. Ellerby
London
1803

Joseph Elliot & Sons
Sheffield
1890 c. ...

Isaac Ellis & Sons
Sheffield

Thomas Turner & Co.
Sheffield
1886 ...

William Hay
Birmingham

S. Evans
Sheffield
1816

Evans & Matthews
Birmingham
1890 c. ...

Fenton & Anderton
Sheffield

Fattorini & Sons
*Bradford, Kirkgate
&Westgate*
1895 c. ...

F. Cobb & Co
Sheffield
1905–1911 c.

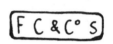

Fenton Brothers Ltd.
Sheffield
1897 ...

Fenton Brothers
Sheffield
1860–1880 c.

Fenton Brothers
Sheffield
1880 c.–1896

Frederick Derry
Birmingham
1867–1891

F.E. Timm & Co.
Sheffield
1877 c. ...

F.E. Timm
Sheffield

	Fenton Brothers *Sheffield* 1883–1888
	Francis Howard *Sheffield* 1890 c. ...
	Howard *Sheffield* 1870–1974
	Frederick Wilson & William Davis *Sheffield* 1870–1883
	Farrow & Jackson *London*
	Fattorini & Sons *Bradford* 1890 c. ...
 	T. Fox & Co. *Sheffield* 1784 (OSP)
	H. Freeth *Birmingham* 1816 (OSP)
	Frogatt, Coldwell & Lean *Sheffield* 1797 (OSP)

45

Michael Hunter & Son
Talbot Works, Sheffield

Arthur E. Furniss
Sheffield
1859 ...

A.E. FURNISS
SHEFFIELD

John Batt & Co.
London

	John Grinsell & Henry Bourne *Birmingham* 1864–1871
	J. Green *Sheffield*
	G. & J. Bushell *Birmingham* 1899 ...
	Gilbert & Spurrier Ltd *Birmingham*
	Gilbert & Spurrier Ltd *Birmingham* 1886 ...
	R. Gainsford *Sheffield* 1808
	Alfred Field & Co. *Birmingham &* *Sheffield*
	George Bishop & Sons *Sheffield* 1890 c. ...
	George Bowen & Son Birmingham 1877–1890

George Bishop & Sons
Sheffield
1894–1940

Gotscher & Co.
Birmingham

Gotscher & Co.
Birmingham

G. Deakin & Co.
Sheffield

G.E. Hawkins
Birmingham
1887 ...

George Hawksley &
Co.
Sheffield

G. Harrison
Birmingham
1823

G. Harrison
Sheffield
1823

George Hawksley & Co.
Sheffield
1864 ...

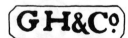

	George Hawksley & Co. *Sheffield*
	G. Lee & Co. *Sheffield* 1888–1967
	George Richmond Collis & Co. *Birmingham* 1848–1868
	George Richmond Collis & Co. *Birmingham* 1869 c.–1893
	George Shadford Lee *Sheffield* 1879–1900 c.
	George Goodfellow & Sons *London* 1882 ...
	G. Teasdell *London*
	George Travis & Co. *Sheffield* 1863 ...
	G. Unite *Birmingham*

George Ward
Sheffield

George Wish
Sheffield
1879 ...

R. Gainsford
Sheffield
1808

W. Garnett
Sheffield
1803

John Blyde
Clintock Works,
Sheffield

G. Gibbs
Birmingham
1808

William Gibson & Co.
Ltd.
Belfast
1896 ...

J. Gilbert
Birmingham
1812

J. Gilbert
Birmingham
1812

 J. Gilbert
Birmingham
1812

 John Gangee
*The Glaciarium,
Middlesex*

 GLORIOUS. Edwin Lander & Co.
Birmingham

 N.C. Reading & Co.
Birmingham

 Edwin Fear
Bristol

 Goldsmiths' Alliance
Ltd
London

 The Goldsmiths &
Silversmiths Co. Ltd
London
1898 ...

 Goodman, Gainsforth
& Fairbairn
Sheffield
1800

 E. Goodwin
Sheffield
1795

Spurrier & Co. *London*	 **GORDON SILVER**
J.G. Graves *Sheffield* 1900–1914	J. G. GRAVES E P N S S
Benjamin Grayson & Son *Sheffield* 1871 ...	**B.GRAYSON&SON** **SHEFFIELD**
R. & J. Walsham *Birmingham*	**THE** **GREAT EASTERN**
J. Green *Birmingham* 1807	
J. Green & Co. *Birmingham* 1799	
W. Green & Co. *Sheffield* 1784	
Barker Brothers *Birmingham*	*CRIEL NICKEL SILVER*
Griffiths & Browett *Birmingham* 1862	

Doughty, Alexander & Co.
Liverpool

J. & J. Drysdale & Co.
London

I. Guide & Co.
Sheffield
1895 c. . . .

H

D. & G. Holy
Sheffield
1821

Harold & Ashwin
Birmingham
1868 ...

Hukin & Fenton
Birmingham

Jonathan Wilson Hukin
& John Thomas Heath
Birmingham
1875 ...

Joseph Hirons &
Henry Hodson Plante
Birmingham
1860–1863

W. Hutton
Sheffield
1839

William Hutton & Sons
Sheffield & London

William Hutton & Sons
Sheffield & London

William Hutton & Sons
Sheffield & London

	Archer & Company *Sheffield*
	Archer, Machin & Marsh *Sheffield*
	Henry Atkin *Sheffield* 1823
	Atkin Brothers *Sheffield* 1868 ...
	Atkin Brothers *Sheffield* 1853 ...
	Henry Bourne *Birmingham* 1896 ...
	Harrison Brothers & Howson *Sheffield* 1862–1909
	Harrison Brothers & Howson *Sheffield* 1862 c.–1896
	Harrison Brothers & Howson *Sheffield* 1897 ...

Haseler Brothers
Birmingham
1884–1887

Hammond, Creake & Co.
Sheffield
1886–1935

HC&Co.S
5856

Hawksworth, Eyre &
Co.
Sheffield
1850 c.–1873

Hawksworth, Eyre &
Co.
Sheffield
1853–1867

Hawksworth, Eyre &
Co. Ltd.
Sheffield
1874 ...

Hawksworth, Eyre &
Co.
Sheffield
1892–1894

Hawksworth
Sheffield
1894–1911

Harrison Fisher
Sheffield
1898 ...

H. Freeth
Birmingham
1816

 H. Fisher & Co.
Sheffield
1900–1920

 H.G. Long & Co.
Sheffield
1890 c. ...

 Harrison Brothers &
Howson
Sheffield

 Harrison Brothers &
Howson
Sheffield

 Henry Hall
Birmingham
1829

 Walker
Sheffield
1868–1916

 Henry Hobson & Sons
Sheffield & London
1889 c. ...

 Henry Hodson Plante
& Co.
Birmingham
1882–1896

 James Howarth & Sons
Sheffield

H

Henry Millington Harwood
& Henry Holdson Plante
Birmingham
1887–1892

Hardman, Powell & Co.
Birmingham
1883 ...

Boardman
Sheffield
1861–1927

Harwood, Plante &
Harrison
Birmingham
1883–1886

Joseph Hirons, Henry
Hodson Plante & Co.
Birmingham
1863–1882

Henry Rogers, Sons &
Co.
Sheffield
1897 ...

H. Schurhoff & Co.
Birmingham

Tudor & Leader
Sheffield
1760   (OSP)

Tudor & Leader
Sheffield
1760   (OSP)

	Horace Woodward & Co. *Birmingham* 1876–1893
	Henry Wilkinson & Co. Ltd *Sheffield* 1872–1892
	Henry Wilkinson & Co. *Sheffield* 1862 c.–1872
	Henry Wilkinson & Co. *Sheffield* 1843–1871
	Henry Wilkinson & Co. Ltd *Sheffield* 1872–1894
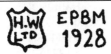	Henry Wilkinson & Co. Ltd *Sheffield* 1872–1894
	Horace Woodward & Co. Ltd *Sheffield* 1894 …
	W. Hall *Birmingham* 1820
	George Walker & Henry Hall *Sheffield* 1891 c. …

59

H

W. Hall
Birmingham
1820 (CP)

Joseph Hancock
Sheffield
1755 (OSP)

**IOS^{H} HANCOCK
SHEFFIELD.**

M. Hanson
Sheffield
1810 (OSP)

G.W. Harris & Co.
Sheffield
1845–1863

**G.W.HARRIS & C^{O}
SHEFFIELD**

J. Harrison
Sheffield
1809 (OSP)

Harrison
Sheffield
1843–1865

HARRISON
NORFOLK WORKS
SHEFFIELD
2746

Harrison & Howson
Sheffield
1862–1909

James Dixon & Sons,
Harrods
Sheffield & London
1890 c. ...

Henry Millington
Harwood & Son
Birmingham
1892–1894

60

	Aaron Hatfield *Sheffield* 1808 c. (OSP)
	Aaron Hatfield *Sheffield* 1810 c. (OSP)
G & J W HAWKSLEY	George Hawksley & Co. *Sheffield* 1852 c.–1879 c.
	Hayman & Company *Birmingham*
JOSEPH HAYWOOD&COMPY MANUFACTURERS.SHEFFIELD	Joseph Haywood & Co. *Sheffield* 1890 c. …
	Henry Brooks & Co. *London*
HERALD TRUMPETER	C.A.E. Speyer & Co. *London*
HESSIN.	Andrew Charles *Birmingham*
	S. Hibbert & Son *Sheffield* 1900–1909

William Marples & Sons *Sheffield*		
Higginson Robinson *Liverpool*		
D. Hill & Co. *Birmingham* 1806		
J. Hinks *Birmingham* 1812		
J. Hipkiss *Birmingham* 1808		
J. Hobday *Birmingham* 1829		
Henry Holdsworth & Sons *Sheffield* 1864–1900		
H. Holland & Co. *Sheffield* 1784		
D. & G. Holly *Sheffield* 1821		

	Dan Holly, Parker & Co. *Sheffield* 1804
	Dan Holly, Wilkinson & Co. *Sheffield* 1784
	H.H. Vivian & Co. Ltd. *Birmingham*
	J. Horton *Birmingham* 1809
	D. Horton *Birmingham* 1808
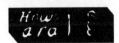	S. & T. Howard *London* 1809
HOWARD SHEFFIELD	Francis Howard *Sheffield* 1890 c. ....
HUNTER SHEFFIELD	Michael Hunter & Sons *Sheffield* 1884–1887
	W. Hutton *Birmingham* 1807

H

EPNS MAKERS' MARKS

W. Hutton
Birmingham
1837 (CP)

W. Hutton
Birmingham
1831 (CP)

I. & I. Waterhouse
Sheffield
1833

John Bell
Sheffield

Creswick & Co.
Sheffield
1858–1863

John Gilbert
Birmingham
1876 ...

Joseph Hancock
Sheffield
1755

J. Harrison & Co.
Sheffield
1866–1891

G. Lees
Birmingham
1811

J. Knowles & Son
Sheffield

John Littlewood
Sheffield
1772

Mappin & Co.
Royal Cutlery Works,
Sheffield

John Oxley
Sheffield

J.P. Cutts
Sheffield

J. Rowbotham & Co.
Sheffield
1768   (OSP)

Israel Sigmund
Greenberg & Co.
Birmingham
1895 ...

John Winter & Co.
Sheffield
1765   (OSP)

Frederick Whitehouse
Lion Works,
Birmingham

Frederick Whitehouse
Lion Works,
Birmingham

N.C. Reading & Co.
Birmingham

 Daniel & Arter
*Globe Nevada Silver
Works, Birmingham*

 Perry & Company Ltd
Birmingham

 Walter J. Ramsbottom
Vine Works, Sheffield

 IXION G.E. Walton & Co. Ltd
Birmingham

James & Charles
Tidmarsh
London
1886 c.–1899

J. & J. Bell
Sheffield

John Biggin
Sheffield

Biggin, John
Sheffield

J. Bradbury
Sheffield
1889–1892

John Bodman
Carrington
London
1880 ...

J.B. Chatterley & Sons
Ltd.
Birmingham
1896 ...

Thomas Bradbury &
Sons
Sheffield
1863–1867

Jonas & George Bowen
Birmingham
1859–1877

	Jonathan Bell & Son *Sheffield* 1897 c. ...
	Jonas Bowen & Sons *Birmingham* 1877 ...
	Thomas Bradbury & Sons *Sheffield*
	James Chesterman & Co. maker of measuring tapes *Sheffield* 1862 ...
	J. Collyer & Co. Ltd *Birmingham* 1900 ...
	John Clarke & Sons *Sheffield* 1895 ...
	Creswick *Sheffield* 1853–1855
	Johnson, Durban & Co. Ltd *Birmingham* 1897 ...
	James Deakin & Sons *Sheffield* 1871–1890 c.

James Deakin & Sons
Sheffield
1871–1898

James Deakin & Sons
Sheffield
1890 c. ...

James Dixon & Sons
Sheffield
1869 c.–1879 c.

James Dixon & Sons
Sheffield
1879 ...

James Dixon & Sons
Sheffield

James Dixon & Sons
Sheffield
1848 c.–1869 c.

James Dixon & Sons
Sheffield
1848–1878

James Dixon & Sons
Sheffield
1848–1878

James Dixon & Sons
Sheffield
1879–1935 c.

J.E. Bushell
Birmingham
1891 ...

 Joseph Elliot & Sons
Sheffield
1890 c. ...

 James Fenton
Birmingham

 James Fenton
Sheffield

 James Fenton
Sheffield
1868–1875

 James Fenton
Sheffield
1875–1883

 Joseph Gilbert
Sun Works,
Birmingham

 John Gough
Birmingham
1870–1885 c.

 John Gilbert & Sons
Birmingham &
London
1894 ...

J

John Grinsell & Sons
Birmingham
1892 ...

John Harrison
Sheffield
1843–1866

John Hardman & Co.
Birmingham
1845–1875

John Hoyland & Co.
Sheffield
1764   (OSP)

J.H. Hunt
Birmingham
1887–1898

J. Hawksworth
Sheffield
1867–1911

J.H. Hunt & Co.
Birmingham
1898 ...

T. & J. Creswick
Sheffield
1811   (OSP)

John Hoyland
Sheffield
1764   (OSP)

 691	Harrison *Sheffield* 1843–1865
	Potter *Sheffield* 1884–1890
	J. Slate & Son *Sheffield*
	Hale Brothers *Sheffield*
	Hawksworth *Sheffield* 1873–1892
	Hawksworth *Sheffield* 1873–1892
	Mappin & Son *Sheffield*
	John Morton & Co. *Sheffield & London*
	J. Needham *Sheffield*

J. North
Sheffield

John Neal & Co.
London
1873–1880 c.

John Neal & Co.
London

J. Nodder
Sheffield
1890 c.–1904

John Nowill & Sons
Sheffield
1867–1889

James Pinder & Co.
Sheffield
1890 c. ...

James Pinder & Co.
Sheffield
1877–1894

J. Roberts
Sheffield

Joseph Rodgers & Sons
Sheffield

	Joseph Rodgers & Sons *Sheffield*
	John Round & Son Ltd *Tudor & Arundel* *Works, Sheffield*
	Joseph Rodgers & Sons *Sheffield* 1822 (OSP)
	Joseph Rodgers & Sons *Sheffield* 1822
	Joseph Rodgers & Sons *Sheffield* 1858–1871
	Joseph Rodgers & Sons *Sheffield* 1871 ...
	John Round & Sons Ltd *Sheffield* 1863–1897
	John Round & Sons Ltd *Sheffield* 1874–1896
	John Round & Sons Ltd *Sheffield* 1880 c.–1896

75

John Round & Sons
Ltd
Sheffield
1897 ...

John Round & Sons
Ltd
Sheffield
1872–1957
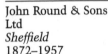

John Round & Sons
Ltd
*Tudor & Arundel
Works, Sheffield*

Josephus Smith
Sheffield

J. Smallwood
Sheffield
1823   (OSP)

J. Dixon
Sheffield
1848–1878

Jacob & Samuel
Roberts
Sheffield
1765   (OSP)

John Sherwood & Sons
Birmingham
1858–1896

John Sherwood & Sons
Birmingham
1897 ...

J. Thompson
Sheffield

J. Thompson
Sheffield

J. Turton & Co.
Sheffield
1898–1909

J. Turton & Co.
Sheffield
1910–1923

James Tidmarsh
London

J. Townroe
Sheffield
1887–1916

J. Turton & Co.
Sheffield
1898–1923

Towndrow Brothers
Sheffield

J.W

W. F. Wostenholme
Sheffield

Joseph Wilmore
Birmingham
1807   (OSP)

James Walter Tiptaft
Birmingham
1886 ...

J. Y. Cowlishaw
Sheffield

John Yates & Sons
Birmingham

J Y & S

John Yates & Sons
Birmingham
1879 ...

John Yates & Sons
Birmingham

John Yates & Sons
Birmingham

Daniel & Arter
*Globe Nevada Silver
Works, Birmingham*

James Jay
London
1867–1897

**JAY
366 ESSEX ROAD
LONDON**

C. JOHNSON & CO. SHEFFIELD	Cristopher Johnson & Co. *Sheffield* 1896 ...
	J. Johnson *Sheffield* 1812
	Jones *Birmingham* 1824
	T. Jordan *Sheffield*

Alfred F. Kleinwort &
Percy W. Peerless
London
1895–1896

Alfred F. Kleinwort &
Percy W. Peerless
London
1897 ...

Levetus Brothers
Birmingham

"KARANTI SILVER"

GOLDTECTA

"ECLIPSE SOVEREIGN PURSE"

Kendal & Dent
London
1883 ...

Levetus Brothers
Birmingham

S. Kirkby
Sheffield
1812

Kirby, Beard & Co. Ltd
Birmingham &
Redditch
1897 ...

	Lingard & Baker *Birmingham* 1871 ...
	Lee & Middleton *Sheffield*
	George Shadford Lee & Henry Wigfull *Sheffield* 1871–1898
	George Shadford Lee & Henry Wigfull Ltd *Sheffield* 1899 ...
	George Shadford Lee & Henry Wigfull *Sheffield* 1879–1898
	Levesley Brothers *Central Works,* *Sheffield*
	Levesley Brothers *Central Works,* *Sheffield*
	Lockwood Brothers Ltd *Sheffield*
	Levesley *Sheffield* 1875 c.–1935

Levesley
Sheffield
1875 c.–1935

J. Law & Son
Sheffield
1807

(OSP)

John Law
Sheffield
1810 c.

(OSP)

R. Law
Sheffield
1807

(OSP)

Thomas Law
Sheffield
1758

(OSP)

Thomas Law
Sheffield
1758

(OSP)

Thomas Law
Sheffield
1758

(OSP)

Daniel & Arter
*Globe Nevada Silver
Works, Birmingham*

A. C. Lea
Sheffield
1808

(OSP)

LEE & COMPY **ELECTRO PLATE** **SHEFFIELD**	Lee, White & Co. *Sheffield* 1886–1887
	George Lees *Birmingham* 1811 c. (OSP)
	George Lees *Birmingham* 1811 (OSP)
LEVIATHAN.	John James & Sons *Victoria Works,* *Redditch*
LIFE	Francis John Townsend *Sheffield*
	John Lilly *Birmingham* 1815 (OSP)
	Joseph Lilly *Birmingham* 1816 (OSP)
LINDER FEARNLEY SHEFFIELD	Linder Fearnley *Sheffield* 1851–1852
ALFRED LINDLEY **SHEFFIELD**	Alfred Lindley *Sheffield* 1883–1896

M. Linwood & Sons
Birmingham
1808　(CP)

J. Linwood
SBirmingham
1807　(CP)

J. Linwood
Birmingham
1807　(CP)

W. Linwood
Birmingham
1807　(CP)

Michael Hunter & Son
Talbot Works, Sheffield

Lockwood Brothers Ltd.
Sheffield
1898 c. ...

LOCKWOOD BROTHERS SHEFFIELD

J. Love & Co. and
Love, Silverside, Darby
& Co.
Sheffield 1785 c.　(OSP)

Love, Silverside, Darby
& Co.
Sheffield
1785 c.　(OSP)

	Joseph Mappin & Brothers *Sheffield*
	Mackay & Chisholm *Edinburgh*
	Joshua Maxfield & Sons *Sheffield* 1894 ...
	Mappin & Webb *Sheffield & London* 1897 c. ...
	Mappin Brothers *Queens Works, Sheffield & London*
	Mappin Brothers *Queens Works, Sheffield & London*
	M. Beal *Sheffield*
	McLean Brothers & Rigg Ltd *London*
	William Mammat, George Albert Buxton & Co. *Sheffield 1865–1867*

M

Richard Morton
Sheffield
1765

Richard Morton
Sheffield
1765

M. de J. Levy & Sons
London

Richard Martin
Sheffield
1854–1897

Richard Martin,
Ebenezer Hall & Co.
Sheffield
1854 ...

Richard Martin,
Ebenezer Hall & Co.
Sheffield
1860 c.–1896

Richard Martin
Sheffield
1880–1934

Richard Martin,
Ebenezer Hall & Co.
Sheffield
1895 c. ...

James McEwan & Co.
Ltd
London

Mappin, Webb & Co.
Sheffield

 Mappin, Webb & Co.
Sheffield
1861–1890

 Willis
Sheffield
1872–1885

**HERBERT MACLAURIN
SHEFFIELD** Herbert Maclaurin
Sheffield
1894 ...

 F. Madin & Co.
Sheffield
1788

 Fisher
Sheffield
1900–1925

 Mappin Brothers
Sheffield
1848–1863

MAPPIN BROS Mappin Brothers
*Queens Works,
Sheffield & London*

 Mappin Brothers
Sheffield
1865–1905

87

Mappin Brothers *Sheffield* 1850	**MAP PIN** **BRO THERS**
Mappin Brothers Sheffield 1863–1894 c.	**MAPPIN-BROTHERS** **222, REGENT STREET** **AND** **LONDON-BRIDGE**
John Newton Mappin & George Webb *Sheffield & London* 1866–1871	**MAPPIN & WEBB** **77 & 78 OXFORD ST** **71 & 72 CORNHILL** **LONDON**
John Newton Mappin & George Webb *Sheffield & London* 1871–1880 c.	**MAPPIN & WEBB** **76, 77 & 78 OXFORD ST** **& MANSION HOUSE** **BUILDINGS, CITY** **LONDON**
Mappin & Webb *Sheffield* 1887 ...	**MAPPIN & WEBB'S** **PRINCE'S PLATE,** **R⁹ 71552**
Mappin & Webb *Sheffield & London* 1887 c. ...	**MAPPIN & WEBB** **PRINCES' PLATE**
Mappin & Webb Ltd. *Sheffield & London* 1899 c. ...	**MAPPIN & WEBB'S** **PRINCES PLATE** **LONDON & SHEFFIELD**
Mappin & Webb *Sheffield* 20th Century	MAPPIN & WEBB London & Sheffield MAPPIN PLATE 🛡 W 20252 ⅙ PINT
W. Markland *Sheffield* 1818	(OSP) **W · MARKLAND**

	Bramwell, Brownhill & Co. *Sheffield*
MATTHIAS SPENCER & SONS	Spencer, Matthias & Sons *Sheffield*
	S. Maw, Son & Thompson *London*
	Samuel Hancock & Sons *Mazeppa Works, Sheffield*
	H. Meredith *Sheffield* 1807
	John Baker & Company *Wheeldon Works, Sheffield*
	James Tidmarsh *London*
	George Bishop & Sons *Sheffield* 1890 c. ...
	Swann & Adams *Canada Works, Birmingham*

J. Moore
Sheffield
1784

J. Moore
Sheffield
1784

F. Moore
Sheffield
1820

Lockwood Brothers Ltd
Sheffield

S. Mordan & Co.
London

R. Morton & Co.
Sheffield
1785

H.D. Muir & Co.
London

	John Neal & Co. *London*
	Platnauer Brothers *Bristol*
	Nathaniel Smith *Sheffield* 1756 (OSP)
N.W.	Norton & White *Birmingham* 1883–1899
	Needham, Veall & Tyzack *Sheffield* 1890 c. ...
	W.S. Savage & Co. *Sheffield*
NEAL'S PYRO SILVER	John Neal & Co. *London*
	C. Needham *Sheffield* 1821 (OSP)
	William Milner & Sons *Leek*

Henry Wilkinson &
Co. Ltd
Sheffield

Daniel & Arter
*Globe Nevada Silver
Works, Birmingham*

F.R. Martino
Birmingham

W. Newbould & Son
Sheffield
1804 (OSP)

John McLeownan
McMurtrie
Glasgow

J. Nicholds
Sheffield
1808 (OSP)

Matthias Spencer &
Sons
Sheffield
1880 c. ...

John Nodder & Sons
Sheffield
1863 ...

JOHN NODDER
& SONS
SHEFFIELD

John Nodder & Sons
Sheffield
1863–1904

5
JOHN NODDER
& SONS
SHEFFIELD
🄱🄰🄴🄣
2352

O

	Osborn & Elliot *Sheffield*
	T. Oldham *Sheffield* 1860
	Slack & Grinold *Bath Works, Sheffield*
	H. Schurhoff & Co. *Birmingham*
T. OTLEY **SHEFFIELD**	Thomas Otley & Co. *Sheffield* 1846 c.–1860
THOMAS OTLEY **SHEFFIELD**	Thomas Otley & Co. *Sheffield* 1861–1875
THOMAS OTLEY **& SONS** **SHEFFIELD**	Thomas Otley & Sons *Sheffield* 1876–1888

Pembrook & Dingley
Birmingham
1883–1886

Pembrook & Dingley
Birmingham
1887–1898

Parkin & Marshall
Telegraph Works,
Sheffield

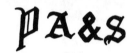

Philip Ashberry &
Sons
Sheffield
1856–1890 c.

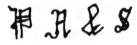

Philip Ashberry &
Sons
Sheffield
1861–1890

Philip Ashberry &
Sons
Sheffield
1880 c. ...

Philip Ashberry &
Sons
Sheffield
1867–1935

Philip Ashberry &
Sons
Sheffield
1880–1935

Philip Ashberry &
Sons
Sheffield

Payton & Co.
Birmingham

Padley, Parkin & Co.
Sheffield

Padley, Parkin &
Staniforth
Sheffield
1855 c.–1880 c.

J. Prime
Birmingham
1839

Padley, Staniforth &
Co.
Sheffield

The Potosi Silver Co.
Birmingham
1878 ...

Pryor, Tzack & Co.
Sheffield

Walker & Hall
Sheffield

RICHARD PARKIN
& SON
SHEFFIELD

Richard Parkin & Son
Sheffield
1853–1872

Thomas Parkin
Sheffield
1839–1871

J. Parsons & Co.
Sheffield
1784   (OSP)

L. & C. Glauert
Sheffield

Pinder Brothers
Sheffield
1923–present

Peake
Sheffield
1807   (OSP)

A. & F. Pears
London & Middlesex

R. Pearson
Sheffield
1811   (OSP)

Pemberton & Mitchell
Sheffield
1817   (OSP)

Hawksworth, Eyre &
Co.
Sheffield

PERUVIAN SILVER	Hands & Sons *Birmingham*
	Jackson Petfield *Sheffield* 1876
	C. Jones *Liverpool*
	Samuel Pimley *Birmingham* 1810 c.
	Piston Freezing Machine & Ice Co. *Middlesex*
	John Derby & Sons *Sheffield*
	The Potosi Silver Co. *Birmingham*
	The Potosi Silver Co. *Birmingham*
	Potter *Sheffield* 20th Century

John Henry Potter *Sheffield* 1884 …	

J. Prime *Birmingham* 1839	(CP)	

J. Prime *Birmingham* 1839	(CP)	

J. Prime *Birmingham* 1839	(CP)	

Thomas Prime & Son *Birmingham* 1844 c.–1894	

Thomas Prime & Son *Birmingham*	

John Neal & Co. *London*	**PYRO GOLD**

 Samuel Roberts &
Charles Belk
Sheffield
1863 ...

 Roberts & Briggs
Sheffield

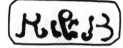 Rose & Brough
Birmingham
1894 ...

   Roberts
Sheffield
1864–1867

 Roberts
Sheffield
1864–1867

 Roberts
Sheffield
1892–1920 c.

 Roberts & Briggs
Sheffield
1860

 Roberts
Sheffield
1916–1919

 Roberts
Sheffield
1920–1923

R

Roberts & Hall
Sheffield

Roberts & Slater
Sheffield

Samuel Roberts &
Joseph Slater
Sheffield
1845–1858

Roberts Smith & Co.
Sheffield
1828   (OSP)

Rhodes Brothers
Sheffield

William Hutton &
Sons
Sheffield & London

A. Hodd & Sons
Middlesex

Richard Hodd & Son
London
1872–1896

Martin, Hall & Co.
*Shrewsbury Works,
Sheffield*

R.M. Johnson & Co.
Sheffield
1890 c. ...

R.M. Johnson & Co.
Shoreham Plate Works, Sheffield

Robert Pringle & Co.
London
1882 ...

Richard Richardson
Sheffield
1873–1900 c.

Richard Richardson
Sheffield
1895 ...

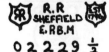

Richard Richardson
Sheffield
1873–1924

Rylands
Sheffield
1876–1910 c.

Ridge, Woodcock & Hardy
Sheffield
18765–1880

W.R. Humphreys & Co.
Sheffield

101

Willaim Daffern
Birmingham

Openshaw & Co.
Birmingham &
London

John Ridal
Paxton Works, Sheffield

Frederick Barnes & Co.
London, Birmingham
& Sheffield

John Sherwood & Sons
Birmingham

Bramwell, Brownhill &
Co.
Sheffield
1891 ...

Frederick Derry
Birmingham
1867–1891

Theophilus Richards
& Co.
Birmingham

Richard Richardson
Sheffield
1873–1900 c.

Joseph Ridge & Co.
Sheffield
1880–1884

Roberts Cadman & Co.
Sheffield
1785 (OSP)

J. S. Roberts
Sheffield
1786 (OSP)

Joseph Rodgers & Sons
Sheffield
1822 (OSP)

RODGERS

Joseph Rodgers & Sons
Sheffield

RODGERS
CUTLERS
TO HER
MAJESTY
ORIGINAL & GENUINE PLATE

Joseph Rodgers & Sons
Sheffield

Joseph Rodgers & Sons
Sheffield

JOSEPH RODGERS & SONS

Joseph Rodgers & Sons
Sheffield

V ♛ R
JOSEPH RODGERS & SONS
CUTLERS TO HER MAJESTY.
✳ ✢

Joseph Rodgers & Sons
Sheffield

Joseph Rodgers & Sons
Sheffield
1860–1970

Joseph Rodgers & Sons
Sheffield

RODGERSINE

Joseph Rogers & Sons
Birmingham
1819

ROGERS

Henry Rogers, Sons &
Co.
Sheffield
1897 ...

HENRY ROGERS, SONS & Cᵒ CUTLERS SHEFFIELD

Rosing Brothers & Co.
London

ROSING

Frederick Derry
Birmingham

"ROYAL STANDARD"

Frederick Derry
Birmingham

"ROYAL STANDARD"
VICTORIA
SILVER

W. Ryland & Son
Sheffield
1807

RYLAND

John Nodder & Sons
Sheffield
1894 c. ...

 Sansom & Creswick
Sheffield

   Sansom & Creswick
Sheffield

 Arthur Elwell Spurrier
& Co.
London
1886 ...

 James Shaw & Fisher
Sheffield
1872–1894

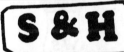 Slater, Son & Horton
Sheffield

 Stacey, Henry &
Horton
Sheffield

 Slack Brothers
*Leicester Works,
Sheffield*

    S. Bright & Co.
Sheffield

Sturges, Bladdon &
Middleton
Birmingham
1884 ...

S. Colmore
Sheffield
1790

Samuel Evans & Sons
Birmingham
1875 ...

Fenton
Sheffield
1888–1891

S.F. Evans & Co.
Birmingham
1894 ...

Fenton
Sheffield
1891–1896

S. & T. Howard
Sheffield
1809

Sheffield Plate Co.
Sheffield
1884

Roberts
Sheffield
1867–1879

Fenton Mathews & Co.
Sheffield
1760   (OSP)

Selig, Sonnenthal & Co.
London

Thomas Bradbury & Sons
Sheffield
1858–1896

W. & S. Ward
Manchester

H. Samuel & Sons
Manchester

Harriet Samuel
Sheffield
1880 c. ...

T. Sansom & Sons
Sheffield
1821

SAVARS.

Evans, Lescher & Webb
London

SAVARS.

Evans Sons & Co.
Liverpool

Adey Bellamy Savory & Sons *London* 1854–1866	
Howell & James Ltd *London*	*The "Sceptre"* *"Jubilee"*
W. Scott *Birmingham* 1807 (CP)	
James Shaw & Fisher *Sheffield* 1833–1894	**SHAW & FISHER** **SHEFFIELD**
James Shaw & Fisher *Sheffield* 1872–1894	**SHAW&FISHER** **43 SUFFOLK ROAD** **SHEFFIELD**
Alfred R. Ecroyd *Sheffield* 1884–1890	
J. Shephard *Birmingham* 1817 (CP)	
R. Binnall & Co. *Shrewsbury*	THE SHROPSHIRE AND NORTH WALES GENERAL SUPPLY STORES 35 PRIDE HILL, SHREWSBURY. R BINNALL & C? PROPRIETORS.
Hawksworth, Eyre & Co. *Sheffield*	**Siberian Silver.**

 **SIBERIAN SILVER**	Hawksworth, Eyre & Co. *Sheffield*
	R. Silk *Birmingham* 1809
	W. Silkirk *Birmingham* 1807
	Potter *Sheffield* 1884–1940
 **SILVENE**	Henry Fielding *Birmingham*
	John Yates & Sons *Birmingham*
	Maurice Baum *Sheffield*
	Maurice Baum *Sheffield*
	William Page & Co. *Birmingham*

Arthur Heckford
Egerton
Birmingham

John Yates & Sons
Birmingham

John Yates & Sons
Birmingham

William Rae & Co.
Liverpool

John Ingram
Birmingham

W.R. Box & Co.
Dublin

Hutton
Sheffield
20th Century

T. Small
Birmingham
1812

I. Smith
Birmingham
1821

	W. Smith *Sheffield* 1812	
	Smith & Co. *Sheffield* 1784	
	Smith, Tate, Nicholson & Hoult *Sheffield* 1810	(OSP)
	J. Smith *Sheffield* 1836	
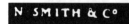	N. Smith & Co. *Sheffield* 1784	
	J. Smith & Son *Sheffield* 1828	
	Walker & Hall *Sheffield*	
	Mason Brothers Ltd *London*	
SOUTHERN & RICHARDSON SHEFFIELD	Southern & Richardson *Sheffield* 1887–1900 c.	

S

Spencer, Matthias &
Sons
Sheffield

John Batt & Company
London

William Spurrier
Birmingham
1850 c.–1887

SPURRIER

Ebenezer Stacey &
Sons
Sheffield
1870 c.–1900 c.

**E. STACEY & SONS
SHEFFIELD**

Ebenezer Stacey
Sheffield
1843–1856

**E. STACEY
SUCCESSOR TO
I. VICKERS
BRITANNIA PLACE
SHEFFIELD**

Ebenezer Stacey & Son
Sheffield
1857–1900 c.

**E. STACEY
& SON
SUCCESSORS TO
JOHN VICKERS
BRITANNIA PLACE
SHEFFIELD**

George Wheeler
Birmingham

Frederick Derry
Birmingham

Frederick Derry
Birmingham

**"STANDARD"
VICTORIA
SILVER**

Staniforth, Parkin & Co.
Sheffield
1784

William T. Staniforth
Ascend Works,
Sheffield

Steam Electro-Plating & Gilding Co.
Southampton

Keep Brothers
Birmingham

B. Stot
Sheffield
1811

SUNLIGHT

Lever Brothers
Port Sunlight

Muirhead, James & Co.
Glasgow

Sykes & Co.
Sheffield
1784

SYLFERET.

Roberts & Belk
Furnival Works,
Sheffield

Thompson & Brown *Sheffield*	
T. Badger & Co. *Sheffield*	
Thomas Bradbury & Sons *Sheffield* 1867–1878	
Thomas Bradbury & Sons *Sheffield* 1858–1863	
Thomas Bradbury & Sons *Sheffield* 1892–1916	
Thomas Bradbury & Sons *Sheffield* 1853–1857	
T. Butts *Birmingham* 1807	
T.W. Eaton *Sheffield*	
T. Ellis *Plymouth*	

T. Freeman
Sheffield

Thomas Goodfellow
London
1873–1893

Thomas Goodfellow
London
1893 ...

Thomas Hardwood &
Sons
Birmingham
1864–1896

Thomas Harwood
Birmingham
1845–1864

Creswick
Sheffield
1852–1853

Thomas Latham &
Ernest Morton
Birmingham
1866–1896

Thomas Latham &
Ernest Morton
Birmingham
1897 ...

T. Land
Sheffield
1901–1919

T. Marples
Sheffield

T.P. Lowe
Sheffield

Thomas Otley & Sons
Sheffield
1889 c.–1900

T. Royle
Sheffield

W.R. Nutt & Co.
Sheffield
1894 ...

Ridge, Woodcock &
Hardy
Sheffield

Thomas Turner
Sheffield

Thomas Turner & Co.
Suffolk Works,
Sheffield

Thomas Turner & Co.
Sheffield
1886 ...

Thomas Turner & Co.
Sheffield
1865–1885 c.

Thomas Thorold
Sturtevant
London
1871 ...

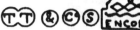

Thomas Turner & Co.
Sheffield
1883–1940

Tudor & Leader
Sheffield
1760

(OSP)

Thomas Woolley
Birmingham
1887–1897

Thomas Woolley
Birmingham
1898 ...

Thomas Wilkinson &
Co.
Birmingham
1844 c.–1875 c.

Thomas White & Co.
Birmingham
1893 ...

Thomas Wilkinson &
Sons
Birmingham
1875 c. ...

Taunton & Johnnson
Birmingham
... 1885 c.

Needham, Veall &
Tyzack
*Eye Witness Works,
Sheffield*

Lloyd, Taylor & Co.
London

S. Thomas
Sheffield
1818

E. Thomason &
Dowler
Birmingham
1807

E. Thomason &
Dowler
Sheffield
1807

Tonks & Co.
Sheffield
1824

Samuel Tonks
Birmingham
1807

Albert Samuel Bradley
Sheffield

TOPAZ

	James Schoolbred & Co. *Middlesex*
	Aluminium Co. Ltd *London*
	Armstrong, Stevens & Son *Birmingham*
	Creswick *Sheffield* 1852–1890
	Daniel & Arter *Globe Nevada Silver Works, Birmingham*
	Gotscher & Company *Birmingham*
	William Mather *Manchester*
	Thomas Otley & Sons *Sheffield* 1889–1900 c.
	Planters' Stores & Agency Co. *London*

N.C. Reading & Co.
Birmingham

Roberts & Belk
Sheffield
1895–1920 c.

Van Wart, Son & Co.
Birmingham

Henry Barnascone &
Son
Sheffield
1884 ...

Levetus Brothers
Birmingham

Frederick Newton &
Co.
London

Thomas White
Birmingham

Mappin & Webb
Sheffield & London
1899 c. ...

Mappin
Sheffield
1873 ...

	Mappin *Sheffield* 1900 ...
	Newton, Francis & Sons *Portobello Works, Sheffield*
	Tudor, Leader & Nicholson *Sheffield* 1784 (OSP)
	S. Turley *Birmingham* 1816 (OSP)
	J. Turton *Birmingham* 1820 (OSP)
	J. Turton *Birmingham* 1820 (OSP)
	John Tyler *Sheffield* 1836–1869 (OSP)
	J. Tyndall *Birmingham* 1813 (CP)

William Whiteley
Middlesex

UNIVERSAL PROVIDER.

Vale Brothers &
Sermon
Birmingham
1884 ...

 Van Wart, Son & Co.
Birmingham

VALARIUM

KENDULAM

John Round & Son
Ltd.
*Tudor & Arundel
Works, Sheffield*

 N.C. Reading & Co.
Birmingham

VICTORY

Henry Rossell & Co.
Sheffield

 VENTURE

Slater Brothers
Sheffield

Phosphor Bronze Co.
Southwark, Surrey

George Waterhouse &
Co.
Sheffield

George Waterhouse &
Co.
Sheffield
1842

Wilson & Davis
London & Sheffield

Wilson & Davis
London & Sheffield

Watson
Sheffield
1897–1940

George Walker &
Henry Hall
Sheffield
1861 ...

George Walker &
Henry Hall
Sheffield
1862–1896

Walker
Sheffield
1861–1890

Walker
Sheffield
1852–1897

W. & M. Dodge
Manchester

 George Waterhouse &
Co.
Sheffield

 William Arthur Smith
Benson & Co.
London
1898 ...

 W. Brearley
Sheffield

 W. Briggs
Sheffield
1823

 William Batt & Sons
Sheffield
1895 c. ...

 W.C. Cox
Birmingham
1878 ...

 William Clarke
London
1885–1888

 W. & M. Dodge
Manchester

Perry & Company Ltd
Birmingham

W. E. W.

W.F. Casewell
Birmingham
1893 ...

W.F.C

W. F. Wostenholme
Sheffield

W.F.W

W.F. Wostenholme
Sheffield
1858–1870

W.F.W.

William Gallimore &
Co.
Sheffield

W.G

William Gallimore &
Co.
Sheffield
1864–1887

WG

William Gough
Birmingham
1849–1870

William Hutton &
Sons
Sheffield & London

William Henry Lyde
Birmingham
1881 ...

William Hutton & Sons
Sheffield
1864–1886 c.

William Hutton & Sons
Sheffield
1849

William Hutton & Sons
Sheffield & London

William. Hutton
Sheffield
1849

William James Myatt & Co.
Birmingham
1900 ...

Walker, Knowles & Co.
Sheffield

Lee, William & Sons
Sheffield

W. Morton
Sheffield

William Mammat & Sons
Sheffield
1879–1895

William Marples &
Sons
Sheffield
1883 c.–1896

William Marples &
Sons
Sheffield
1897 ...

William Page & Co.
Birmingham
... 1896

Parkin & Marshall
Telegraph Works,
Sheffield

William Page & Co.
Birmingham

William Page & Co.
Birmingham
... 1896

William Page & Co.
Birmingham
1897 ...

Taylor & Company
Swansea

W.R. Humphreys &
Co.
Sheffield
1889 c. ...

	W.R. Nutt & Co. *Sheffield* 1894 ...
	William Sissons & George *Sheffield & London*
	William Spurrier & Co. *Birmingham* 1889 ...
	Sissons *Sheffield* 1858–1885
	Stratford, W & H *Sheffield*
	William Suckling & Sons *Birmingham* 1895 ...
	Shirtcliffe *Sheffield* 1921–1931
	Robert Pringle & Co. *Wilderness Works, Middlesex*
	W.W. Harrison & Co. *Montgomery Works, Sheffield*

W.W. Harrison & Co.
Montgomery Works,
Sheffield

W.W. Harrison & Co.
Montgomery Works,
Sheffield

William Wheatcroft
Harrison
Sheffield
1857–1896

White, Henderson &
Co.
Elcho Works, Sheffield

White & Johnstone
Sheffield

Walker & Hall
Sheffield
1878 c. ...

Walker & Hall
Sheffield
1893 c. ...

Walker & Hall
Sheffield
1891–1909

Walker & Hall
Sheffield
1910–1970

 J. Waterhouse & Co.
Sheffield
1807 ⓄⓈⓅ

 J. Waterhouse & Co.
Sheffield
1833 c. ⓄⓈⓅ

 Waterhouse, John,
Hatfield, Edward &
Co.
Sheffield 1836 c. ⓄⓈⓅ

 Watson, Fenton &
Bradbury
Sheffield
1795 ⓄⓈⓅ

  Watson, Pass & Co.
(Late J. Watson)
Sheffield
1811 ⓄⓈⓅ

WWATSON
MAKER
SHEFFIELD

W. Watson
Sheffield
1883 ⓄⓈⓅ

 WATTS & HARTON
LONDON

Watts & Harton
London
1854 c. ...

WILLIAM WEBSTER
SYCAMORE WORKS

William Webster
Sheffield
1880 c. ...

 Bonser & Son
London

Francis Howard
Aberdeen Works,
Sheffield

John Blyde
Clintock Works,
Sheffield

W. Hipwood
Birmingham
1809

J. White & White &
Allgood
Birmingham
1811

Thomas White
Sheffield
1866–1892

William Whiteley
London
1885 c. ...

W. WHITELEY
WESTBOURNE GROVE
BAYSWATER

Wignall Heeley & Co.
Sheffield
1895 ...

WIGNALL HEELEY & CO.
SHEFFIELD

Henry Wilkinson &
Co.
Sheffield
1836 c.

Joseph Willmore
Birmingham
1807 c.

	Joseph Willmore *Sheffield* 1807
WITHIN **THE REACH OF** **ALL.**	Birts & Son *Woolwich*
	Needham, Veall & Tyzack *Sheffield* 1890 c. ...
	Needham, Veall & Tyzack *Eyewitness Works,* *Sheffield*
	W. Jervis *Sheffield* 1789
WOSTENHOLME & BIGGIN 117 MATILDA STREET SHEFFIELD	Wostenholme & Biggin *Sheffield* 1876–1879
	W. Woodward *Birmingham* 1814
	S. Worton *Birmingham* 1821
	J. Wright & G. Fairbairn *Sheffield* 1809

Ellis Newton
Birmingham

Parkin & Marshall
Telegraph Works,
Sheffield

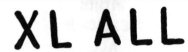

John Copley & Sons
Richmond Works,
Sheffield

Henry Hobson & Sons
Sheffield & London
1889 c. ...

Y & S	John Yates & Sons *Birmingham*
Y **V S**	John Yates & Sons *Birmingham*
YATES & SONS	John Yates & Sons *Birmingham*
YATES **VIRGINIAN SILVER**	John Yates & Sons *Birmingham*
YATES'S **VIRGINIAN**	John Yates & Sons *Birmingham*
	John Yates & Sons *Birmingham*
J. YATES & SONS	John Yates & Sons *Birmingham*
J **YATES** **&SONS**	John Yates & Sons *Birmingham*
JOHN YATES & SONS	John Yates & Sons *Birmingham*

S. & C. Young & Co.
Sheffield
1813

Arrow

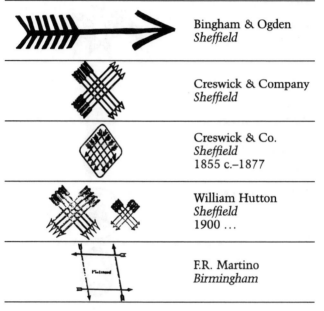

Bingham & Ogden
Sheffield

Creswick & Company
Sheffield

Creswick & Co.
Sheffield
1855 c.–1877

William Hutton
Sheffield
1900 ...

F.R. Martino
Birmingham

Anchor

Wells, Gallimore &
Taylor
Birmingham

Pictures

Bat

John Batt & Co.
London

Bell

Roberts, Smith & Co.
Sheffield
1828   OSP

William & George
Sissons
Sheffield
1858 ...

Smith, Sissons & Co.
Sheffield
1848

Sissons
Sheffield
1858–1891

Belt

Charles Rowe
Courtney
Middlesex

Bird

	S. Brittain & Co. *St George's Works, Sheffield*
	Alfred Field & Co. *Birmingham & Sheffield*
	Alfred Field & Co. *Birmingham & Sheffield*
	Hukin & Heath *Birmingham*
	Ellis Newton *Birmingham*
	Jonathan Wilson Hukin & John Thomas Heath *Birmingham* 1889 c. ...
	The Potosi Silver Co. *Birmingham* 1878 ...
	Waterhouse Hatfield & Co. *Sheffield* 1886 (OSP)

Bird (cont.)

Thomas Wilkinson
Birmingham
1868 ...

Blacksmith

Charles Smith
Sheffield

Boar

J. & J. Beal
*Redhill Works,
Sheffield*

Boy

A. & F. Pears
London & Middlesex

Butterfly

John Morton & Co.
Sheffield & London

Centaur

Carl Maigatter
London

Compasses

William Jackson & Co.
*Sheaf Island Works,
Sheffield*

Cooper

Cooper Brothers &
Sons Ltd
Sheffield
1896 c. ...

Cross

Joseph Rodgers & Sons
Ltd.
Sheffield
1900 c. ...

Cupid

John Grinsell & Sons
Birmingham
1879 ...

John Grinsell & Sons
London

Deer

George Reid & Co.
London

Dragon

John Batt & Co.
London

Dragon (cont.)

John Batt & Co.
London

Elephant

William Meyerstein &
Co.
London

Fan

Carl A. Von Der Meden
London

Figure

John Batt & Co.
London

Henry Bourne
Birmingham
1877 ...

Pictures

Figure (cont.)

John Dyson
Leeds

John S. Elmore & Co.
London

Speyer, Schwerdt &
Co.
London

Fish

Not attributed
1760

Flag

Philip Ashberry &
Sons
Sheffield

Henry Rogers, Sons &
Co.
Sheffield
... 1896

Fleur-de-Lys

Atkin
Sheffield
1890 ...

William R. Deykin &
Sons
Birmingham
1892–1895

William R. Deykin &
Walter A. Harrison
Birmingham
1895 ...

Richard Hodd &
William Linley
London
1862–1872

Flower

Maurice Baum
Sheffield
1891 ...

Rosing Brothers & Co.
London

Rosing Brothers & Co.
London

Pictures EPNS MAKERS' MARKS

Globe

Daniel & Arter
*Globe Nevada Silver
Works, Birmingham*

Gong

James Deakin & Sons
Sheffield
1871–1900 c.

James Deakin & Sons
Sheffield
1890 c. ...

Hand

Padley, Parkin & Co.
Sheffield
1849

Padley, Parkin & Co.
Sheffield
1849–1855 c.

Padley, Parkin &
Staniforth
Sheffield
1855 c.–1880 c.

Hand (cont.)

John Watson & Son
Sheffield
1830

Head

A. Hodd & Sons
Middlesex

Horn (Animal)

George Bowen & Sons
Birmingham
1890 c. ...

William Webster
Sheffield
1880 c. ...

Horn (Musical)

James Dixon & Sons
Sheffield
1879 ...

Horn (Musical) (cont.)

James Dixon & Sons
Sheffield
1886 c. ...

James Dixon & Sons
Sheffield
1890 c. ...

Michael Hunter &
Sons
Sheffield
1884–1887

Horse

I. Guide & Co.
Sheffield
1895 c. ...

Hale Brothers
Sheffield
1885 c. ...

Hale Brothers
Sheffield

Moenich, Oscar & Co.
London

Pictures

Horse (cont.)

Henry Rogers & Sons
Co.
Sheffield &
Wolverhampton

Insect

Lewis Barnascone
Sheffield

Kangaroo

Robert Sorby & Sons
Sheffield
... 1898

Kettle

Joseph Haywood & Co.
Sheffield
1890 c. ...

Pictures

Key

Atkin Brothers
Sheffield
1895 c. ...

Nowill, John & Sons
Sheffield

Henry Wilkinson &
Co.
Sheffield
1836

Henry Wilkinson &
Co.
Sheffield
1855 c.–1892

Knight

S. Brittain & Co.
*St George's Works,
Sheffield*

Henry Knight & Co.
London

Lamp

Samuel Roberts &
Charles Belk
Sheffield
1863 ...

Lion

Charles Howard
Collins
Birmingham
1895 c. ...

Charles Howard
Collins
Birmingham

Koerber & Co.
London

Donald & Co.
Birmingham & Whitby

Oscar Moenich & Co.
London

Pictures

Mermaid

Perry & Co. Ltd
Birmingham

Number

Robert Winter
Sheffield

2216

Orb

Blagden, Hodgson
Sheffield
1821

Walker, Knowles & Co.
Sheffield
1840

Pipe

G. Wostenholm & Son
Ltd
Washington Works,
Sheffield

Pictures

Plough

Samuel York & Co.
Wolverhampton

Scales

Meriden Britannia Co.
London

Sheep

Henry Brooks & Co.
London

Shield

Army & Navy Co-op
Society Ltd
Westminster

Philip Ashberry &
Sons
Sheffield
1880 ...

Shield (cont.)

R. Sutcliffe & Co.
Sheffield
1786

Thomas Hands
Birmingham
1899 ...

Signpost

William Suckling
Birmingham
1895 ...

Star

M. Boulton & Co.
Sheffield
1784

Frederick Whitehouse
Lion Works,
Birmingham

Pictures

Sun

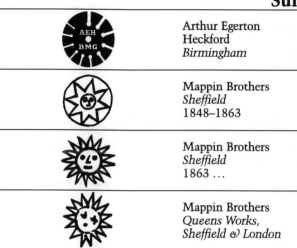

Arthur Egerton
Heckford
Birmingham

Mappin Brothers
Sheffield
1848–1863

Mappin Brothers
Sheffield
1863 ...

Mappin Brothers
*Queens Works,
Sheffield & London*

Sword

Garfitt, Thomas &
Son
*Cross Scythes Works,
Sheffield*

Long, Hawksley & Co.
*Hallamshire Works,
Sheffield*

H.G. Long & Co.
Sheffield
1880 c. ...

Sword (cont.)

Robert Pringle & Co.
London
1882 ...

Target

Francis Howard
Sheffield
1890 ...

Tree

Patrick O'Connor
Lancashire

Trident

Joseph Ridge & Co.
Sheffield
1880–1884

Joseph Ridge; John
Round & Sons Ltd
Sheffield
1886 ...

Violin

George Ibberson
Sheffield

Wheatsheaf

Co-op Wholesale
Society Ltd
Manchester

Wheelbarrow

Henry Bolsover
*Portland Works,
Sheffield*

Others

Allen & Martin
Birmingham

Jonathan Bell
Sheffield

Others (cont.)

Charlton Brothers
Birmingham

John Goode & Sons
Birmingham

Gotscher & Co.
Birmingham

J.V. Hope &
G.F.W. Hope
*Atlantic Works,
Wednesbury & London*

Levy Brothers
London

J.S. Manton & Co.
Birmingham

Merzbach, Lang &
Fellheimer
London

John Nodder & Son
Sheffield